SLAM! STARS OF WRESTLING

JEFF HARDY

BOUND FOR GLORY

TRACY BROWN

rosen publishing's
rosen central

New York

For Kieran

Published in 2012 by The Rosen Publishing Group, Inc.
29 East 21st Street, New York, NY 10010

First Edition

Library of Congress Cataloging-in-Publication Data

Brown, Tracy.
Jeff Hardy: bound for glory/Tracy Brown.
    p. cm.—(Slam! stars of wrestling)
Includes bibliographical references and index.
ISBN 978-1-4488-5537-7 (library binding)—
ISBN 978-1-4488-5599-5 (pbk.)—
ISBN 978-1-4488-5600-8 (6-pack)
1. Hardy, Jeff—Juvenile literature. 2. Wrestlers—United States—Biography—Juvenile literature. I. Title.
GV1196.H316B76 2012
796.812092—dc23
[B]
                                                                    2011022623

Manufactured in the United States of America

CPSIA Compliance Information: Batch #W12YA: For further information, contact Rosen Publishing, New York, New York, at 1-800-237-9932.

CONTENTS

Introduction...4

1 Childhood Days...7

2 Going Pro...16

3 Living on the Edge...23

4 Exit and Return...28

5 Outside of the Ring...34

Timeline...39

Glossary...41

For More Information...42

For Further Reading...44

Bibliography...46

Index...47

INTRODUCTION

Jeff Hardy has become one of the most known and most successful wrestlers in World Wrestling Entertainment (WWE). Beyond wrestling, he is a musician, a poet, an artist, a motocross racer, a husband, and a father.

He and his brother, Matt Hardy, were truly self-made. They were dealt their first real blow as little boys, when their mother died of brain cancer. They were raised by their dad, who encouraged and supported his energetic, rambunctious sons all through their childhoods.

It was their dad who bought them the trampoline on which they used to imitate the moves of the WWF (as the WWE was called at the time) wrestlers they admired on television. Jeff's dad also bought him his first motocross bike, which led to a lifelong love of motocross racing.

Watching their dad work hard and raise them single-handedly instilled in Jeff and his brother a work ethic that has helped the siblings achieve success in many areas. The brothers created their own wrestling organization, OMEGA, because they had no other venue in which to wrestle. They caught the attention of the WWE and went on to become one of the best-known wrestling duos, before pursuing solo careers.

Jeff Hardy leaps from a ladder to land on his brother, Matt, during an extreme rules match at WrestleMania XXV, at the Reliant Stadium on April 5, 2009, in Houston, Texas.

Had she lived, Jeff and Matt's mother would certainly be very proud of her sons' achievements and of the job their father did raising them alone. Their drive, ambition, dedication, and down-to-earth manner has brought them a lot of success, in the ring and in other areas, too.

You know Jeff Hardy from the ring, but this book will help you get to know the man behind the wrestling persona. Hardy is a dominating force in the ring, but he's also got a sensitive side that he shares through his art, music, and poetry. These hobbies help keep him balanced and keep him from burning out as he has in the past. He expresses himself very openly and honestly, making him not such an enigma at all, other than to wonder how he manages to juggle all of his interests and commitments.

1 CHILDHOOD DAYS

Jeff Hardy was born on August 31, 1977, in Cameron, North Carolina, to Gilbert and Ruby Moore Hardy. Jeff was one of two sons. His older brother, Matthew, also grew up to be a professional wrestler. Jeff's mother died of brain cancer when he was only nine years old. He and his brother were then raised by their father.

Both Jeff and his brother were always big fans of wrestling as children, and it gave them something to bond over with their dad. As Jeff recalled in a PWS Forums interview, "Our dad would take us to Fayetteville, and that was the closest access to professional wrestling. We always wanted to go back to our closest venue to our home and actually be the performer instead of the spectator." Coincidentally, the boys grew up with Shannon Moore and Gregory Helms, who also became professional wrestlers like the Hardy brothers.

Jeff and Matt's father bought his sons a trampoline when they were kids. They used it to create a makeshift wrestling ring in their backyard. The boys started imitating the moves they saw on television. The boys emulated the Rockers (Shawn Michaels and Marty Jannetty) and were drawn to the exciting high-impact, aerial style.

Macho Man Randy Savage was one of their favorite wrestlers. Michael P. S. Hayes, whom the boys later ended up working with in the WWF, was also one of their favorites.

Growing up, Jeff was also very interested in motocross racing, and his father bought him his first bike when he was twelve. He had his first race at age thirteen, and he continues to participate in motocross racing today. Jeff was always athletic and played baseball, too, until an arm injury he got in a motocross crash meant he had to stop. In high school, he was a fullback and linebacker on the football team and briefly competed in amateur wrestling. Jeff was also a very good student, and his favorite subjects were U.S. history and art.

Hard Work Pays

The Hardy brothers were always hard workers, and Jeff credits his upbringing in Cameron with helping him develop his work ethic at an early age. "We grew up farming tobacco until my dad went full time in the Postal Service," Jeff said in a PWS interview. "We were pretty much working [extremely hard], like farming tobacco, and we really got a good idea what it was like to take part in hard labor at a very young age. I think that made us really strong in our lives to grow up doing something that not many kids are ever around, and like living out in the country is such a blessing."

Jeff Hardy gets a boot in the face from his brother, Matt, during an extreme rules match at WrestleMania XXV. The two are often rivals.

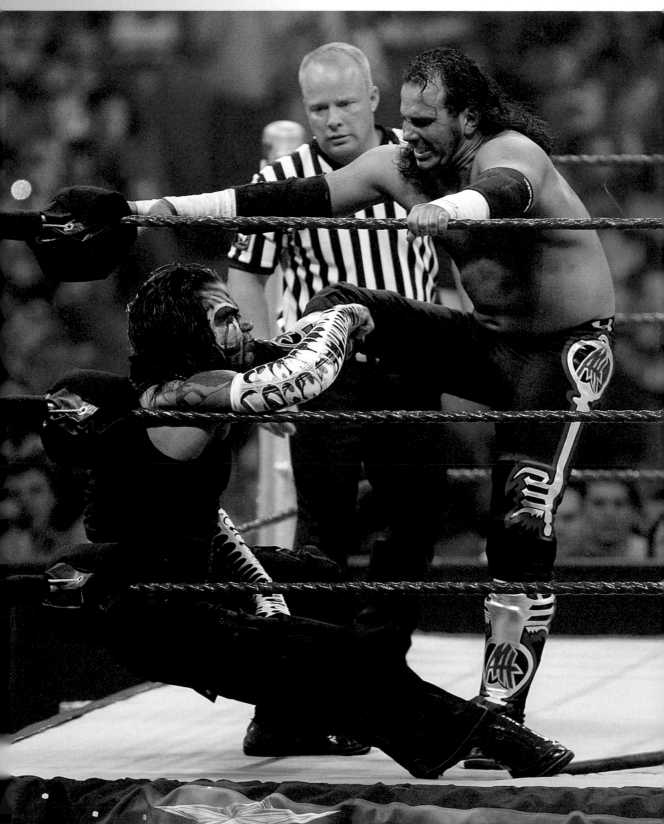

Jeff is so proud of his childhood town that, unlike other guys who become successful and move to faraway cities, he continues to prefer Cameron. In the same PWS interview, Jeff said he will always think of Cameron as his home. "To this day, I love it," he said. "I couldn't imagine living in some city or any other state or whatever. I remember there was a time before Matt and I made it and I said, 'Oh yeah, when I make it, I want to move out to L.A. or Hollywood or somewhere big.' But now that I've seen these different choices, it really is 'There's no place like home.' And Cameron is my home and that's forever."

Paving Their Own Way

Jeff has always been very ambitious. He began his affiliation with the World Wrestling Federation (WWF) when he was just sixteen years old. He had a job as a wholesaler of wrestling equipment. Both boys knew they wanted to be part of professional wrestling, and they worked really hard—often for no pay and with little result—just to be around wrestling. In an online interview on PWS Forums, Jeff recalled that his father wasn't always in support of the boys' wrestling ambitions and often felt they were putting too much into it and getting nothing back.

Jeff said the only way he could convince his father that he and his brother could make it as wrestlers was to actually make it as wrestlers. Jeff's dad couldn't always understand the hours the boys would spend driving to events just to get the chance to wrestle, without earning any money from it. The boys would also suffer injuries in the ring, and their dad, while wanting to support them, often suggested they try to find a more steady form of employment, something a little more stable. But when they finally did become successful wrestlers, Jeff said it meant the world to his father.

Jeff Hardy credits his father for instilling a strong work ethic in him and his brother. When the boys were young, their father put them to work farming tobacco.

As Jeff told IGN UK, the brothers also sometimes lost faith in themselves, but they always managed to stick it out. There were times when they doubted themselves and really struggled to survive financially. But Jeff said that even in the rough times when he was landscaping for money and Matt was running around looking for sponsors for their shows, somewhere in the back of his mind, he knew it would happen. Now that he and his brother are so successful, Jeff reflects on the harder times, and he says it just played out like it was supposed to.

OMEGA

Although Jeff and his brother loved to wrestle, there were not many opportunities for wrestling where they lived. There was no local organization in which the boys could hone their skills and get the promotion required to make a name for themselves. Not to be discouraged, the boys decided to form their own wrestling organization.

The boys founded the Organization of Modern Extreme Grappling Arts (OMEGA) in 1997. OMEGA stood apart from other wrestling promotions of the time because it focused more on high-flying and hardcore wrestling in its shows. High-flying wrestling is a style that involves maneuvers in which the wrestler springs or thrusts himself into the air while using the posts and ropes of the ring for support. The maneuvers are dangerous, and because of the injuries that can be sustained, not all organizations allow high-flying wrestling. Hardcore wrestling allows the use of props that would not be considered legal in traditional wrestling.

Because the OMEGA style of wrestling was unusual and extremely entertaining, the promotion was a quick success. It also had great talent: OMEGA featured several wrestlers who went on to have strong careers, including

COSTUME DESIGNERS

Although the boys started their own wrestling promotion with OMEGA, they did not have the funds needed to buy expensive, showy costumes that they needed when in character for wrestling. A lot of what gets noticed about wrestlers is their character, and a major part of establishing character, and catching the attention of the audience, is the clothes worn in the ring. The boys again showed how industrious they could be to overcome this hurdle: Matt Hardy simply took it upon himself to design and make their own costumes. It's hard to imagine the powerful Hardy boys sitting down to sew their own outfits, but it is another example of how much work they were willing to put into their dream of becoming WWE stars. It also illustrates how much their characters are their own vision and how much ownership they have both taken over their careers, even back when stardom and success were a mere pipe dream.

Shannon Moore, Joey Mercury, Christian York, Joey Abs, Steve Corino, Generation Me, C.W. Anderson, Gregory Helms, and of course, the Hardy brothers.

Big Break

Jeff Hardy's big payback came in 1998 when he caught the attention of the WWF (now the WWE) and was signed to a contract with the organization. The boys were both trained by Dory Funk Jr., along with Kurt Angle, Christian, Test, and A-Train. The boys got their start as jobbers. Jobbers are wrestlers

Kurt Angle is a professional wrestler who is currently contracted with Total Nonstop Action Wrestling. Kurt won the gold medal in the heavyweight class at the 1996 Olympics.

whose job it is to lose matches. It doesn't sound like a lot of fun, but it's how many wrestlers get their start. After jobbing for about five months, Jeff and Matt Hardy appeared on television for the first time. They were introduced as an acrobatic wrestling tag team called the Hardy Boyz.

Since then, Jeff's career has taken off, both as part of the Hardy Boyz and in the individual wrestling circuit as well. Throughout his remarkable story of ambition and achievement, Jeff has kept grounded. As he said in a *Wrestling Forum* interview, he never forgets where he came from to get where he is today. To Jeff it is a very important rule: don't ever forget where you started. Always consider yourself human and remain down to earth. Treat your fans with the respect they deserve, and you'll get all that back in the long run.

2 GOING PRO

After signing with the WWE in 1998, Jeff and Matt Hardy formed a tag team, which is kind of like professional wrestling's version of doubles in tennis. The WWE Tag Team Champion has been a very popular, highly competitive segment of the Raw brand for more than forty years. The first Tag Team Championship title was held by Luke Graham and Tarzan Tyler, who defeated Dick the Bruiser and the Sheik in 1971.

That the Hardy brothers would form a tag team was no surprise. The organizers of the WWE no doubt could not believe their luck when they discovered two highly skilled, physically powerful, and hard-working brothers. Jeff and Matt Hardy had their first major victory as a duo on September 27, 1998. On that night's episode of *Sunday Night Heat*, the Boyz were pitted against Japanese wrestling duo Kaientai, which was the team name of wrestlers Men's Teioh and Shoichi Funaki.

Following this victory, the Boyz began to build a following that admired them for their acrobatic antics in the ring. Acrobatics in wrestling are moves that require jumping, dropping, and other dramatic movements that are eye-catching and entertaining for crowds and supposedly devastating to opponents. The Hardy Boyz built a name for themselves as an extreme acrobatic tag team duo.

Their real success came on June 29, 1999, when they won the World Tag Team Championships, defeating the Acolytes Protection Agency (APA). The APA was a tag team consisting of wrestlers John "Bradshaw" Layfield and

Jeff Hardy *(left)* and Matt Hardy *(right)* went from imitating professional wrestlers in their backyard as kids to becoming one of the most successful tag team wrestling duos in the WWE.

Ron "Faarooq" Simmons. The match took place in Fayetteville, North Carolina. Due to a head injury he had sustained in a previous match, Bradshaw was not initially given medical clearance to wrestle in the match, but after "punching" a security guard, Bradshaw stormed the ring anyway.

The Hardy Boyz were the clear underdogs in the face-off. Wearing simple trousers with belts and T-shirts, Jeff and Matt did not look as intimidating as their opponents, who were shirtless with warriorlike markings on their chests, and who entered the arena carrying their championship belts. The Hardy Boyz stood side by side in ready position as they watched the Acolytes approach.

But if the Hardys were intimidated, it was only an act. Just as the Acolytes neared the ring, Jeff Hardy sprang from the ring and landed in the arms of Faarooq and Bradshaw, catching the Acolytes off guard. Taking advantage of their brief confusion, Matt Hardy did a front flip out of the ring, landing on his opponents and knocking them to the ground. It was the start of a very surprising, highly entertaining match ending in a shocking Hardy Boyz victory. Jeff and Matt lost the title to the Acolytes less than a month later, but their victory truly put them on the WWE map. As the Boyz enjoyed more and more success with the WWE, their own promotion, OMEGA, which they had started just two years before, folded.

Love and Family

Another important thing happened in Jeff Hardy's life in 1999: he met Elizabeth Britt. The couple met in North Carolina and were inseparable almost immediately. Hardy has described it as love at first sight. The couple did not marry until March 9, 2011, but a very big announcement was made a year earlier, news that made it clear how committed and in love the couple really are.

RECALLING CHILDHOOD HEROES

Respect has always been the name of the game for Jeff Hardy. In a March 2007 interview with IGN UK, Jeff recalled one of his favorite WWF moments from childhood, back when he was a spectator watching his heroes on television. "I remember WrestleMania 6 with The Ultimate Warrior against Hulk Hogan," Jeff recalled. "It was so cool to see those guys go in there and the fans getting into the match so much. Warrior got the upset win, but when they hugged at the end and showed respect for one another after all of the buildup of animosity between the two and the fans gave them the standing-O, that was one of the best moments to me. Warrior was always such a weird, methodical type character anyway, but he was coming out of his realm and being human for a moment and hugging Hulk Hogan and hitting him on the back and that's still one of my favorite moments from Wrestlemania. That show of respect."

Hulk Hogan is one of the best-known and best-loved stars of the WWE and starred in the successful reality series *Hogan Knows Best*. He is one of Jeff Hardy's heroes.

On an episode of the online program *The Hardy Show* (thehardyshow. com) in August 2010, Jeff described the pain of losing his mom at a young age and the respect he had for his father, who raised his sons by himself. He went on to explain how Shannon Moore, a fellow wrestler and childhood friend, lost his dad in a car accident and how the loss of a parent was something the boys could really relate to each other about.

"And with that said," he went on, "I have an extremely awesome announcement to make. There is a pregnancy, and what pregnancy is that? It's that of the love of my life, Elizabeth Britt. Jeffrey Nero Hardy and Elizabeth Britt are going to be parents. And that is so exciting to me, because I consider that the second stage of life. When you step up, and you take that responsibility to be a dad, to be a mom—that's when you move up. It's scary, don't get me wrong, but it's so exciting." Jeff became extremely private about the other details of the pregnancy, including not sharing the due date or whether the baby was a boy or a girl. Two months later, on October 29, 2010, Jeff announced on Twitter that he and Beth were the proud parents of a "super cool little girl."

Team XTreme

Getting back to the ring, the Hardy Boyz were on fire in 1999. They had a strong premiere in the WWE and were a force to be reckoned with. But a few changes were in the works. In 2000, the brothers decided to go in a different management direction and hired a friend, known as Lita, to be their manager. The three become known as Team XTreme because of their extreme wrestling techniques.

In January 2000, the brothers began a feud with rivals Brother Ray and Brother Christian, a duo better known as the Dudley Boyz. Throughout the

Tag team duo the Hardy Boyz were defeated by wrestlers Billy Gunn and Chuck Palumbo at a Smackdown! event, March 21, 2002, at the Continental Airlines Arena, East Rutherford, New Jersey.

WWE TAG TEAM CHAMPIONSHIP

While the World Tag Team Championship has been around and highly competitive for decades, going back to the 1970s, the WWE Tag Team Championship is relatively new. Originally called the Unified Tag Team Championship, it began in 2002, but it is one of the most coveted and prestigious titles in wrestling today. The idea for the WWE Tag Team Championship came about because the World Tag Team Championship was exclusive to the Raw brand. SmackDown! general manager Stephanie McMahon created her own tag team championship, which has been held by powerful tag team duos, such as John Morrison and the Miz and Los Guerreros.

year, Team XTreme also engaged in a feud with wrestlers Edge and Christian. A three-way feud erupted, and during this time the Hardy Boyz begin participating in Tables, Ladders, and Chairs matches. This is a style of wrestling that uses props—tables, ladders and chairs, for example, as the name suggests. They had their first Tables, Ladders, and Chairs match against the Dudley Boyz and Edge and Christian during SummerSlam 2000, and the Hardy Boyz lost. Regardless, the Boyz had secured their place in the WWE, and their time as crowd favorites and champions was just beginning.

3 LIVING ON THE EDGE

In 2000, Jeff Hardy was starting to make a name for himself as one of the most fearless and daring wrestlers. Still competing as the tag team wrestling duo the Hardy Boyz, Jeff and his brother Matt performed bold, outrageous stunts in the ring. In fact, Jeff Hardy is so well known for his daredevil stunts, some fans have questioned over the years whether he is a really good wrestler or just a fantastic stunt man. In actuality, Jeff is both a very well trained, skilled athlete and a daring and entertaining acrobatic stuntman.

With so many moves up his sleeve, Jeff Hardy's favorite is what he calls the Swanton Bomb. To perform it, Jeff leaps from the top turnbuckle of the ring, does a three-quarter backflip, and lands on his doomed opponent, back first. The Swanton Bomb is his "finisher." It's the final blow he strikes in a match. He's been using the move throughout his career, and he credits it with winning him the World Heavyweight Championship.

The move features in one of Jeff's all-time favorite wrestling memories. He recalled this favorite moment in a March 2007 interview that appeared in IGN Sports UK. It was the Hardy Boyz's first WrestleMania. Jeff climbed to the top of a big ladder and did a Swanton Bomb through a table that had Bubba Ray was on. Jeff loves watching that clip. It reminds him of the days when he practiced it in his backyard, imagining he was in front of a bunch of fans. And to actually be able to do it in a match was very dreamlike to him.

Matt and Jeff Hardy (the Hardy Boyz) pose with their manager, Lita, at the UPN fall television launch party, September 14, 2000, in Hollywood, California.

When he watches that clip, it makes him proud of what he's accomplished.

In the same interview, Jeff talked about the risks he took when he was younger and the toll it took on his body. "I think I've slowed down quite a bit," he admits. "I don't try or attempt even half of the stuff I used to want to try way back in the day when I was a lot younger."

Receiving a Push

Although Jeff became famous as part of a wrestling duo, his individual skills did not go unnoticed. In 2001, Jeff received what is called a "push." A "push" is when a wrestler is invited into an angle, or a storyline. For Jeff, it was his premiere as a singles competitor. Jeff has been very successful as a solo wrestler. In 2001, he held the WWF Intercontinental (defeating Triple H), Light Heavyweight (defeating Jerry Lynn), and Hardcore Championships (defeating Mike Awesome and Van Dam).

After all of Jeff's success away from the Hardy Boyz duo, a storyline in which the brothers were fighting began. A

Former UFC heavyweight champion Brock Lesnar poses for his fans at a UFC 100 weigh-in, July 10, 2009, at the Mandalay Events Center, Las Vegas, Nevada.

supposed rivalry between the brothers caused a rift, or so the story went. Eventually this fizzled out, and the brothers were back in the ring together. In 2002, the Boyz started a feud with Brock Lesnar, but Jeff continued to shine as a singles competitor, winning his third Hardcore Championship. As he continued to make a name for himself away from his brother, the Hardy Boyz eventually split in 2002.

DON'T TRY THIS AT HOME!

Jeff Hardy has several moves that he likes to use against his opponents. They include Twist of Fate, Poetry in Motion, Double Legdrop to Midsection, Sitout Jawbreaker, Whisper in the Wind (Tumbleweed), Catapult into Quebrad, Flying Clothesline off Barricade, Folding Double Leg Drop, Reverse of Fate, and Back Kick. The Swanton Bomb, however, is his signature move. It's an extremely dangerous maneuver. It's very important to remember that athletes like Jeff Hardy are very well trained in the moves they do in the ring. It's not safe to try these moves yourself! You can be badly injured, or worse. In 2009, a nine-year-old boy died in Brooklyn, New York, while trying to imitate Jeff's Swanton Bomb. The boy fell off his apartment's balcony. The WWE frequently reminds fans not to attempt the wrestlers' stunts at home.

4 EXIT AND RETURN

Jeff Hardy started out 2003 by turning into a heel, which is a bad guy in a wrestling storyline. In the storyline, he attacked fellow wrestlers Rob Van Dam and Shawn Michaels. According to some fans, people liked Hardy so much that nobody really bought him as a heel. Fans continued to cheer for him, even as a bad guy. After about a month, Hardy "redeemed" himself by protecting Stacy Keibler, a female wrestler, from another villain and was a good guy again.

Hardy was then part of a storyline in which he was dating female wrestler Trish Stratus, but an ankle injury sidelined Stratus, interrupting the angle. And then, on April 22, 2003, Jeff Hardy was suddenly released from the WWE.

Released

If Jeff Hardy seemed destined to be on top of the WWE world in 2002, things abruptly changed in 2003. Hardy's play-hard, work-hard, take-risks way of life can work for him or against him. Being busy all the time and keeping a hectic and exhausting workout and traveling schedule took its toll on Hardy.

Like some other famous people who fall under pressure, he tried to keep up by turning to drugs. It was a costly mistake but one that he learned from—eventually.

Jeff Hardy was released in 2003 for what the WWE cited as erratic behavior, alleged drug use, tardiness, and failure to show up to work. Hardy

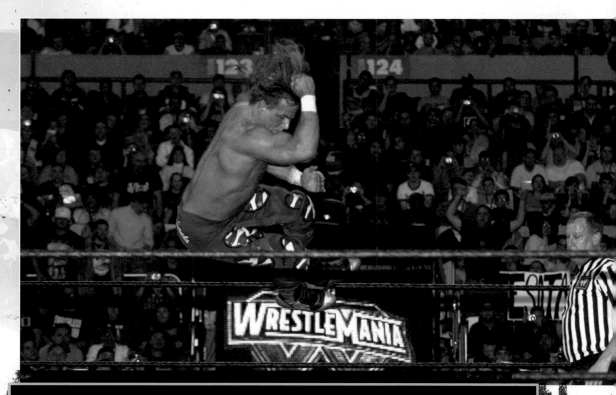

Shawn Michaels prepares to pound his opponent during WrestleMania XX, March 14, 2004. The now-retired Michaels is still contracted to WWE, where he serves an ambassadorial role.

said he was simply burned out, needing a break from all the pressure he was under. Initially Hardy refused to get help. Instead, he accepted the suspension and rejoined the independent circuit. On May 24, 2003, Hardy appeared at an OMEGA event, dressed in a mask and trench coat as his former gimmick, Willow the Wisp. He challenged Krazy K for the OMEGA Cruiserweight Championship, but Hardy lost the match. After being booed during a 2003 Ring of Honor promotion, Hardy took a year off and focused on motocross racing, even building his own track.

No-shows, Suspensions

Hardy returned to the ring at a Total Nonstop Action Wrestling event on June 23, 2004. It was also the premiere of a new character, the Charismatic Enigma, and Jeff used one of his band Peroxwhy?gen's own songs as his entrance music. A month later on July 21, Hardy returned to TNA and was awarded the NWA World Heavyweight Championship. He lost the title to Jeff Jarrett a couple of months later.

Hardy seemed to be making his way back. But things went wrong again. He began showing up late, or not at all, to events. He was eventually suspended from TNA on May 15, 2005, after failing to appear at an event. Hardy said it was because of transportation problems. The suspension was lifted in September, but he was suspended once more in December for again failing to show up at an event and he again cited transportation problems.

Return to WWE

On August 4, 2006, it was announced that Hardy had re-signed with the WWE. He was given another opportunity, and he was happy for it. And soon after, during the November 21 episode of *ECW* on the Sci-Fi Channel, Jeff reunited with his brother, Matt, appearing for the first time in five years as the wrestling duo the Hardy Boyz. Things were looking up again.

But Jeff had not done much to address many of the problems that had gotten him in trouble before. He still overworked his mind and body, he didn't take care of himself, and he again faced burnout.

On March 3, 2008, during an episode of Raw, Jeff Hardy attacked Jericho. An intercontinental title match was organized between Jeff and Jericho on March 10, which Jeff "dropped" to Jericho—a wrestling term for losing as

Jeff Hardy *(left)* and his brother, Matt *(right),* pose for fans at an autographing session at Bookends Bookstore in Ridgewood, New Jersey, January 12, 2007.

part of a script. Offscreen, however, the reasons for Jeff's losing were more serious. He was given a sixty-day suspension, effective March 11, 2008, for his second violation of the WWE drug and substance abuse testing policy.

As Jeff said in an August 2008 interview in *WWE Magazine*, the risk he'd taken was a stupid one, and it cost him dearly. He explained that he was a risk-taker and that sometimes the risks he took were stupid. He had known

TRAGEDY AT HOME

Jeff had even more bad news in 2008 when his house in North Carolina burned to the ground, destroying all of his writings, paintings, and possessions. But by far the most painful loss to Jeff was that of his dog, Jack. Jeff told *WWE Magazine* that losing Jack was the worst part of the whole ordeal. "The one thing I truly wanted to find was my dog's body," he said. "I started by looking in the bedroom, because that's where he always went when he was scared of storms. I looked for two days." Jeff was eventually able to find and bury his dog and was assured by policemen that the dog had not suffered. Jeff and his wife then went to live with his brother, Matt, while they rebuilt. The cause of the fire was electrical.

that there was spot-checking for illegal substances but just chanced it that there would be no testers on the particular day that he was caught. After losing the title to Jericho, Jeff said he exited the ring and apologized to all of his fellow wrestlers. He said they understood and believed it would never happen again.

It had not only cost him the Intercontinental Championship, but it also meant he could not participate in a major match on WrestleMania. He was also under constant watch, being tested two or three times a week. It's a very serious charge in the WWE. Jeff said in the same *WWE Magazine* interview that the whole process of drug testing was humiliating. But as humiliating as this was, it was better than what Jeff originally thought his punishment would be: being fired from the WWE.

Jeff Hardy is met by a swarm of excited fans at the WWE SmackDown! ECW Live event at the Pavilhão Atlântico, Lisbon, Portugal, September 24, 2008. Hardy's fans are important to him.

Jeff told *WWE Magazine* that he is grateful to have such a supportive network of fans who stuck by him after he was suspended. He said he knows there are some people who think he's crazy enough to do drugs again and to risk his career, but that people who think that way only make him stronger. What matters to Jeff is that he knows that his fans and family know him better and understand he has learned that drugs are not a risk worth taking. Jeff pledges to his fans that he will never be suspended again.

5 OUTSIDE OF THE RING

Jeff Hardy is a world-famous professional wrestler, which would be enough of an accomplishment for many people. Hardy's ambition, drive, and natural ability made him a very successful wrestler. He is most known for his work in the ring, but outside of wrestling, Hardy has many other talents and interests. He likes music and art. He is an avid motocross racer. He proves in many areas that if you work hard enough and are passionate about what you do, you can be successful.

The Poet

Hardy has a "tough guy" image, and so for some it may come as a surprise that he's actually got a very sensitive side as well. Poetry is an artistic form that Hardy thinks is very important. It's hard to imagine two activities more different than diving off a ladder in the ring and composing poems, but Hardy has a passion for both.

For Hardy, poetry is a way to express feelings and ideas that he can't convey in another way. His poems do not follow a formal structure, but they do reveal some of his most personal thoughts. They are also a window into his attitudes about life, what he loves, what he regrets, and what he'd like to see change. Hardy calls his poetry "emoetry" because it is written emotion. Here's an example:

If you're lost for words...Become found for actions.
If you're lost in life...Become found with reactions.
Stop searching for who you are...and remember where it started.
You are a flight in motion...Soaring since departed.
Words are a puzzle that will never be completed.
Yours truly... Jeff Hardy.
Ours truly...this life.

The Rockstar

Lots of kids grow up wanting to be WWE wrestlers, and lots of kids grow up wanting to be in rock bands. But very few people actually get to achieve these dreams. Jeff Hardy is one of the lucky ones, as is Shannon Moore, who was once a member of Jeff's band, Peroxwhy?gen.

The band was formed in 2003. They recorded a demo with two songs on it, one of which was called "September Day" and was written to express Hardy's response to the September 11, 2001, terrorist attacks in the United States. Hardy says he's still trying to come up with a name for the type of music his band plays. The closest he can get is a mixture of alternative rock and grunge metal.

Hardy is teaching himself to play guitar and has already taught himself to play the drums. He sings and writes lyrics for the band. The lyrics, like Hardy's poems, are very close to his heart. The band has a very hard, loud sound, but the lyrics are heartfelt and earnest.

The band has not been signed to a record label and has yet to cut a proper album, but they do have a lot of support online, via their MySpace page and the band's Web site. Hardy says the band has about fifteen songs that he feels are finished and good. So it's very possible they will have an official album in the

JEFF HARDY, THE ACTOR?

Jeff Hardy has not pursued a film career like some other wrestlers, such as the Rock and John Cena. But he has appeared on television's *That '70s Show* and *Fear Factor*.

In 2009, it was reported that Hardy would be doing a reality TV show with Fox 21 Studios, to be optioned to networks like MTV. It doesn't appear that the show was ever made, but if you want to get a sense of the "real" Hardy, he released a three-DVD set called *My Life, My Rules*. It includes interviews with Hardy and those who know him best.

Jeff Hardy is seen here in the television series *Fear Factor*, a reality series in which contestants perform dangerous stunts. The Hardy Boyz appeared in a 2002 episode, in which Matt Hardy was the winner.

future. Hardy has never toured with the band but says it's something he might like to do. It's just not easy finding the time to dedicate to all of his interests.

The Motocross Daredevil

Hardy has participated in motocross since he was a kid. His dad gave him his first bike at twelve and was very supportive of his son. Hardy's dad still has all of his motocross trophies in his house.

Hardy considers motocross as challenging and dangerous as wrestling. In fact, he says motocross may even be more dangerous than wrestling because it's hard to keep control of the bike sometimes. With wrestling, you're only dealing with yourself and your own body. In particular, Hardy finds it challenging to jump and control a bike at the same time, but it's the challenge that draws him to the sport. He has to be very careful, though, because motocross can be quite dangerous. If he gets hurt, he can't wrestle, so he's very cautious when he rides.

He recalled in an interview on the Wrestling Forum Web site that, ironically, he broke the only bone he's ever broken doing motocross, not wrestling. "I almost pulled the holeshot out of 40 riders," Hardy recalled, "but after the first turn, I hit a drop off and went sideways and ate it and snapped my collar bone in half." It was only in his second race that he got the injury, but it obviously didn't make him lose interest or confidence in his racing. In fact, during one of his breaks from wrestling, Hardy kept himself busy making his very own motocross track.

The Artist, the Canvas

Hardy is also an artist. He draws, paints, and sculpts. Hardy is also a big fan of tattoos. He says his favorite is the Hardy Boyz symbol that graces his back. It's

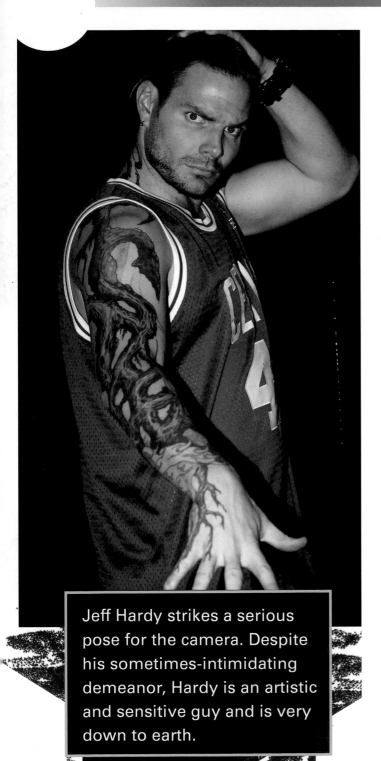

Jeff Hardy strikes a serious pose for the camera. Despite his sometimes-intimidating demeanor, Hardy is an artistic and sensitive guy and is very down to earth.

his favorite because he designed it himself, but also because it represents the careers he and his brother made for themselves as a wrestling duo.

But Hardy's first priority is wrestling. It's important to have hobbies and interests outside of your work, though, even if you have a job that you really enjoy. It's easy to burn out unless you have other outlets to express your emotions, unwind, and discover new talents and interests. Jeff Hardy has had to walk away from wrestling in the past to recover from burnout, and neither he nor his fans want to see that happen again!

1977 August 31, Jeffrey Nero Hardy is born in Cameron, North Carolina.

1986 Jeff's mother dies of brain cancer.

1994 May 24, first WWF match as a jobber against Razor Ramon.

1995 March 25, defeats his brother, Matt, in Robbins, North Carolina, to win the NFWA championship.

1997 Jeff and Matt establish Organization of Modern Extreme Grappling Arts (OMEGA).

1998 Jeff gets his first tattoo, a dragon, which he hides from his father.

1999 February 7, Jeff appears on an episode of *That '70s Show*.

1999 June 29, the Hardy Boyz win the World Tag Team Championship from the Acolytes

1999 October, Jeff and Matt accept contracts from WWE and dismantle OMEGA.

2000 September 24, Unforgiven: Cage Match for Tag Team Title—the Hardy Boyz beat Edge and Christian to become champs.

2001 April 12, Jeff Hardy wins the Intercontinental Championship from Triple H.

2001 July 22, Invasion: Jeff loses the Hardcore Championship to Rob Van Dam.

2002 July 8, Raw: Jeff wins the European Championship from William Regal.

2002 The Hardy Boyz split as a wrestling duo.

2003 January, Jeff briefly becomes a heel.

2003 April 22, Jeff is released from WWE.

2004 June 23, Jeff makes his Total Nonstop Action (TNA) debut.

2006 November 21, the Hardy Boyz reunite.

2007 April 2, Raw: the Hardy Boyz win the World Tag Team Championship by winning a 10-Team Battle Royal.

2008 March 15, Jeff loses his house and his dog in a fire.

2010 August 7, Jeff announces that his girlfriend is pregnant with their first child.

2010 October 28, Jeff Hardy and his girlfriend Elizabeth welcome their daughter, Ruby Moore Hardy.

2011 April 17, Matt Hardy posts a video blog suggesting that Jeff may need back surgery and is considering retirement.

acrobatics Physical stunts or tricks performed in the ring.

angle Fictional plots in wrestling.

call When one wrestler instructs the other about what is going to happen in the match.

championship Acknowledgment that a wrestler is the best in his or her promotion or division in the form of a championship belt.

dropped Surrendering a title as part of a storyline.

feud A rivalry among wrestlers.

gimmick A trademark gesture or action that a wrestler becomes known for.

jobber A wrestler whose job it is to lose to better-known wrestlers.

no-show When a wrestler fails to show up for a match.

OMEGA Organization of Modern Extreme Grappling Arts.

pin In wrestling, to hold an opponent's shoulders to the mat.

push An attempt by a booker to make a wrestler win more matches and be more popular.

storyline A made-up plot in wrestling.

stunts Acrobatics in wrestling, such as jumping or climbing objects.

tag team A pair of wrestlers working together in a tag team match.

WWE World Wrestling Entertainment.

WWF World Wrestling Federation.

Alberta Dirt Riders Association

Lethbridge, AB T1K 6X4

Canada

(780) 416-2977

Web site: http://www.albertadirtriders.com

This Canadian group promotes dirt biking, from providing basic information to beginners to tips for professionals.

International Drug Free Athletics

P.O. BOX 30007

RPO Brooklin Centre

Whitby, ON L1M 0B5

Canada

(905) 655-4320

Web site: http://www.idfa.ca

This Canadian organization is committed to promoting drug-free (natural) bodybuilding worldwide through education, awareness, camaraderie, and community involvement.

National Endowment for the Arts (NEA)

1100 Pennsylvania Avenue NW

Washington, DC 20506

(202) 682-5400

Web site: http://www.nea.gov

The NEA is a nonprofit organization in support of the arts and artists.

National Fire Prevention Association:

1 Batterymarch Park

Quincy, MA 02169

(617) 770-3000

Web site: http://www.nfpa.org

The National Fire Prevention Association is dedicated to preventing accidental fires.

People for the Ethical Treatment of Animals (PETA)

501 Front Street

Norfolk, VA 23510

(757) 622-7382

Web site: http://www.peta.org

PETA aims to prevent and educate the public about animal abuse and mistreatment.

Storm Wrestling Academy

P.O. Box 58013

Chaparral RPO

Calgary, AB T2X 3V2

Canada

Web site: http://academy.stormwrestling.com

Storm Wrestling Academy is a wrestling school operated and taught by former ECW, WCW, and WWE superstar Lance Storm.

Web Sites

Due to the changing nature of Internet links, Rosen Publishing has developed an online list of Web sites related to the subject of this book. This site is updated regularly. Please use this link to access the list:

http://www.rosenlinks.com/slam/jh

FOR FURTHER READING

Amick, Bill. *Motocross America*. Minneapolis, MN: Motorbooks, 2005.

Assael, Shaun. *Steroid Nation: Juiced Home Run Totals, Anti-aging Miracles, and a Hercules in Every High School: The Secret History of America's True Drug Addiction*. New York, NY: ESPN, 2007.

Bales, Donnie. *Pro Motocross & Off-Road Riding Techniques*. Minneapolis, MN: Motorbooks, 2004.

Beekman, Scott. *Ringside: A History of Professional Wrestling in America*. Santa Barbara, CA: Praeger, 2006.

Burns, Christopher, ed. *The Seashell Anthology of Great Poetry*. Edgartown, MA: The Seashell Press, 2011.

Crist, James. *Siblings: You're Stuck with Each Other, So Stick Together*. Minneapolis, MN: Free Spirit Publishing, 2010.

Frederick, Robin. *Shortcuts to Hit Songwriting: 126 Proven Techniques for Writing Songs That Sell*. Auckland, New Zealand: Taxi Music Books, 2008.

Grollman, Earl. *Talking About Death: A Dialogue Between Parent and Child*. Boston, MA: Beacon Press, 2011.

Guitar World Presents Nirvana and the Grunge Revolution. Winonoa, MN: Hal Leonard Corporation, 1998.

Hardy, Jeff and Matt Hardy. *The Hardy Boyz: Exist to Inspire*. New York, NY: It Books, 2003.

Harrison, Charles. *An Introduction to Art*. New Haven, CT: Yale University Press, 2008.

Kaminsky, Michael Sean. *Naked Lens: Video Blogging and Video Journaling to Reclaim the YOU in YouTube*. New York NY: Organik Media, Inc., 2010.

Maddox, Jake. *Motocross Double-cross*. Mankato, MN: Stone Arch Books, 2007.

Madigan, Tom. *Hurricane! The Bob Hannah Story*. Minneapolis, MN: Motorbooks, 2008.

Martino, Alfred. *Pinned*. Boston, MA: Graphia, 2006.

Shields, Brian. *WWE Encyclopedia*. Indianapolis, IN: Brady Games, 2009.

Smith, Harold Ivan. *Grieving the Death of a Mother*. Minneapolis, MN: Augsburg Fortress Publishers, 2003.

Strong, Jeff. *Drums for Dummies*. Indianapolis, IN: Wiley, 2006.

Sullivan, Kevin. *The WWE Championship: A Look Back at the Rich History of the WWE Championship*. New York, NY: Gallery Books, 2010.

Wallace, Rich. *Winning Season*. London, England: Puffin, 2007.

Welker, William. *The Wrestling Drill Book*. Champaign, IL: Human Kinetics, 2005.

Wilson, Jim. *Chokehold: Pro Wrestling's Real Mayhem Outside the Ring*. Bloomington, IN: Xlibris, 2003.

BIBLIOGRAPHY

Barnwell, Bill. "Jeff Hardy Interview." IGN UK Edition. December 18, 2007. Retrieved April 10, 2011 (http://uk.sports.ign.com/articles/842/842317p1.html).

Booboo. "Jeff Hardy Interview." May 10, 2010. Wrestling Forum. Retrieved February 27, 2011 (http://www.wrestlingforum.com/total-nonstop-action-wrestling/504652-new-jeff-hardy-interview.html).

Christensen, Matt. "Rogue Agent." *WWE Magazine*, August 2008. Retrieved April 6, 2011 (http://forum.bodybuilding.com/showthread.php?p=190637371).

Hardy, Jeff, and Matt Hardy. *The Hardy Boyz: Exist to Inspire*. New York, NY: It Books, 2003.

Helmes, Mackenzie. "Jeff Hardy Didn't Deserve His Push." Bleacher Report, January 30, 2010. Retrieved April 30, 2011 (http://bleacherreport.com/articles/336383-jeff-hardy-didnt-deserve-his-push).

Martin, Adam. "Recap of Jeff Hardy interview on the Main Event." June 22, 2010. Retrieved date April 3, 2011. (http://www.wrestleview.com/news2008/1214340818.shtml).

Pantelic, Andrea. "Jeff Hardy Interview." *Up & Coming Weekly*, December 2006. Reprinted at http://www.pwsforums.com/threads/59156-Jeff-Hardy-Interview. Retrieved April 3, 2011.

Robinson, John. "Jeff Hardy Interview." IGN UK Edition. March 27, 2007. Retrieved April 26, 2011 (http://uk.sports.ign.com/articles/776/776337p2.html).

WWE Magazine. "Jeff Hardy Interview." April 7, 2007. Text reprinted at http://www.myspace.com/theenigmajeffhardyfansite/blog/238375989. Retrieved April 1, 2011.

B

Britt, Elizabeth, 18, 20

E

"emoetry," 34–35

F

Fear Factor, 36

H

Hardy, Jeff
  childhood days, 7–15
  exit and return, 28–33
  going pro, 16–22
  introduction, 4–6
  living on the edge, 23–27
  outside the ring, 34–38
Hardy Boyz, 15, 16, 18, 20, 22, 23, 25, 27, 30, 37
Hardy Show, The, 20
Helms, Gregory, 7, 13
Hogan, Hulk, 19

J

jobbers, 13, 15

M

McMahon, Stephanie, 22
Moore, Shannon, 7, 13, 20, 35
motocross, 5, 8, 29, 34, 37
My Life, My Rules, 36

O

OMEGA, 5, 12–13, 18, 29

P

Peroxwhy?gen, 30, 35

R

Raw, 16, 22, 30

S

Savage, Macho Man Randy, 7
"September Day," 35
SmackDown!, 22
SummerSlam, 22
Sunday Night Heat, 16
Swanton Bomb, 23, 27

T

Team XTreme, 20, 22
That '70s Show, 36

V

Van Dam, Rob, 25, 28

W

World Wrestling Entertainment (WWE), 5, 13, 16, 18, 20, 22, 27, 28, 30, 31, 35
World Wrestling Federation (WWF), 5, 7, 10

About the Author

Tracy Brown has written several books for children and young adults on topics ranging from Babe Ruth to the fast food industry and childhood obesity. She lives in the Netherlands.

Photo Credits